IMAGES
of Wales

CENTRAL CARDIFF
THE SECOND SELECTION

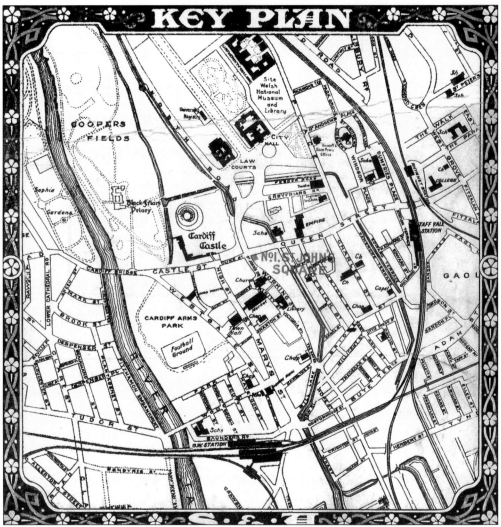

A street plan of Central Cardiff from 1908, with Cardiff Castle in the centre, the Civic Centre to the north, the Arms Park to the south, the River Taff to the west and the gaol to the east. This map is taken from the particulars of the sale by auction of No. 1 St John's Square (marked in the centre) by Messrs Stephenson & Alexander.

IMAGES
of Wales

CENTRAL CARDIFF
THE SECOND SELECTION

Compiled by
Brian Lee

TEMPUS

First published 1999
Copyright © Brian Lee, 1999

Tempus Publishing Limited
The Mill, Brimscombe Port,
Stroud, Gloucestershire, GL5 2QG

ISBN 0 7524 1654 5

Typesetting and origination by
Tempus Publishing Limited
Printed in Great Britain by
Midway Clark Printing, Wiltshire

*'These are days of change,
and the old landmarks are soon blotted out.'*
John Kyrle Fletcher, 1920.

*This book is dedicated to my wife Jacqueline
and is published in the year of our Ruby Wedding Anniversary.*

Contents

Western Mail & Echo Ltd managing director Howard Green (centre) presents thirty-five years service awards to, left to right: Eric Stoker, John Billot, Betty Haywood, J.B.G. Thomas (the then *Western Mail* sports editor) in 1981.

Foreword

When our teacher, George Thomas, who was later to become Speaker in the House of Commons, led us out on our first 'dummy run' to the air raid shelters in the playground of Marlborough Road School in 1940, we never thought that one night the school would be demolished by a direct hit from a German bomber attack. Or that later, when I met George Thomas in the Western Mail & Echo Ltd offices in St Mary Street (before they moved to new headquarters in Havelock Street) that he would remember my face as one of his former pupils. 'Long time ago, but happy days – though none of us had much money!' he laughed. Sir, as we called him (little did we think he would be a lord one day) tried to impart mathematical knowledge to his class of predominantly boneheads; and no doubt that was why when I began to toil for my living, it was with words and as few figures as possible that I did it. Words, working for the *Western Mail*, entailed mainly listening to them and keeping sub-editors' cups topped up with hot tea until the big day when, as a cub reporter (an apprentice reporter), it was over to the Law Courts with Joe Barry (later a top investigative reporter with the *News of the World*). Joe was supposed to show me the ropes. Instead, we found an extra court was sitting and Joe, in his customary ascerbic manner, snapped, 'That's for you, sunshine, you are on your own!'

Suddenly, I found the world was a truly lonely place. But there was always Saturday. That day when the news editor reluctantly released me from the mundane matters to enjoy sports duties. Yipee! Mrs Joliffe Evans would supply a 'cuppa' at half-time at the Bishop's Field, where the great Rex Willis would be playing for Llandaff. Tommy Farr would be fighting at Maindy Stadium and Reg Harris brought his racing bike to the same venue.

There was speedway at Penarth Road, and the Taff Swim in Roath Park Lake and even Glamorgan Cricket at Barracks Field. Like Marlborough Road School, Cardiff Arms Park had taken a direct hit and the upper deck of the north stand and the whole of the west terrace were out of commission for the famous matches by Cardiff and Wales against the Kiwis, the New Zealand army team of 1945/46. Now we have a new Cardiff Arms Park, masquerading under the title of Millennium Stadium. Those who played on, watched at or just talked about, the Arms Park, will still call it that!

So how pleased I am that in *Central Cardiff: the Second Selection*, compiled by my friend and former colleague Brian Lee, tribute is paid, not only to the beloved Arms Park, but also to the Western Mail and Echo Ltd, by way of a series of fascinating photographs.

John Billot
Former sports editor of the *Western Mail*

Introduction

This volume, my second selection of the centre of Cardiff, takes its material from many sources and extends the scope of the first collection. Material for this collection has come from diverse origins and, with the demolishing of the Cardiff Arms Park and the Wales Empire Swimming Pool, I have been fortunate to have been able to include a number of photographs of these one time Meccas of Welsh sport. They will, I am sure, bring back many happy memories to Welsh sportsmen and women.

When Cardiff staged the 1958 Empire and Commonwealth Games they were voted the best games that had yet been held: not since the Cardiff Fine Art, Industrial and Maritime Exhibition of 1896 had the town, or Welsh capital as it is today, staged anything like it.

As a Roath (Cardiff) Harrier I had dreamed of taking part in the marathon event won by the Australian Dave Power. Sadly, for me that is, I wasn't good or fast enough to wear the coveted red vest of Wales. So instead I ended up as a seating steward showing people to their seats! Still, it was a wonderful sporting occasion and I got to meet the world's greatest miler – Herb Elliott. I also got to run on the track when Roath Harriers staged the club three miles championship before the start of the games. But unlike the glorious weather that prevailed for the games it poured down that night and shortly after competing I had to walk the few yards along Westgate Street to work the nightshift on the *Western Mail*.

The *Western Mail* and *South Wales Echo*, then based at St Mary Street, have for more than 100 years provided South Walians with all their news sporting or otherwise, and I am pleased to include a selection of photographs showing some of the staff at work and at play. Working on the production side of things at Thomson House , as a stereotyper for twenty-eight years , when the papers were produced the old hot metal way, gave me a love of words and pictures so I really have to thank *Western Mail & Echo* for my present career as a freelance writer. Finally, as the photographer Peter Narusberg remarked, ' Photographs only come alive when somebody looks at them'. I hope this second selection of Central Cardiff photographs 'comes alive' for you.

Brian Lee
February 1999

One
Cardiff Castle and
Civic Centre

A mulitview postcard of Cardiff Castle from 1955. This multiview postcard illustrates the many facets of the Castle, from the buildings in the centre views, to the state and private rooms on the left and right. Note the beautiful wall paintings and the ornate carving.

Troops from the 3rd Welch Regiment leaving Cardiff Castle at the start of the First World War. This postcard was sold in aid of the National Fund for Welsh Troops which was administered by Countess of Plymouth (president), Mrs Lloyd George (chairman), Sir E. Vincent Evans (treasurer), Mr William Lewis (secretary).

A postcard of Cardiff Castle sent in 1915. The gate to the right of the picture is the same gate as that seen above with the soldiers leaving the castle. Note the gentlemen herding sheep to the right of the tram and the stone animals on the castle wall, as well as the heraldic arms, inset.

The summer smoking room in Cardiff Castle in 1954. Note the painted tiled scenes on the wall above the fireplace.

Prince Charles, hands clasped, is seen inspecting swimming lifeguards at a jamboree held on the Castle Green, shortly after his investiture in 1969.

Duke Street and Castle Street, *c.* 1920. Trams had been running in Cardiff since 1902.

The famous St John's church is to the right of this picture taken from the Castle walls, *c.* 1903.

Cardiff Castle.

A scene from a postcard, depicting the frontage of Cardiff Castle, which was posted in 1904. Horse-drawn trams were still around, but the stone animals adorning the Castle wall and railings (see p. 10) had not yet been installed. Only a lion (possibly the inspiration for later additions) can be seen next to the gate on the right.

The City Hall and Law Courts in 1909. The statue of Gwilym Williams, Stipendiary Judge and Squire (who had died only three years previously), was still to be erected.

The City Hall's Marble Hall contains many statues depicting Welsh heroes. This is a representation of Harri Tewdwr – Henry VII (1457-1509), the first Tudor monarch, and of Welsh royal descent. The statue is by Ernest G. Gillick.

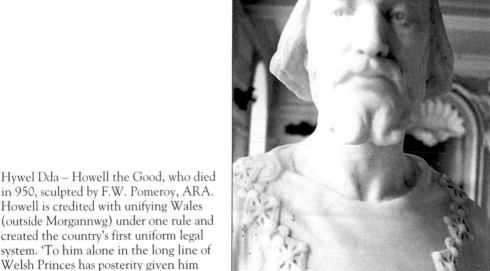

Hywel Dda – Howell the Good, who died in 950, sculpted by F.W. Pomeroy, ARA. Howell is credited with unifying Wales (outside Morgannwg) under one rule and created the country's first uniform legal system. 'To him alone in the long line of Welsh Princes has posterity given him the name of Good' – D. Lleufer Thomas.

CF3   LAW COURTS, CITY HALL AND WELSH NATIONAL MUSEUM. CARDIFF

The Civic Centre complex, including the Law Courts, City Hall and the Welsh National Museum. A man and woman can be seen passing the statue of Judge Gwilym Watkins, Stipendiary Judge and Squire, seen here in the early 1960s.

Owain Glyndŵr – Owen Glendower (1359-1415), inside the City Hall, sculpted by Alfred Turner RBS. Most well known for the representation in Shakespeare's *Henry IV, Part 1*, Glendower is a powerful representative of Welsh nationalism, who rose against English occupation in the early part of the fifteenth century. He was 'a man who fought with splendid courage for the independence of Wales and the advancement of the people' – Owen Rhoscomyl.

15

Llewelyn Ein Llyw Olaf – Llewelyn the Last Prince, who died in 1282. This statue was sculpted by Henry Pegram, ARA. Llewelyn's lineage was recognized by Henry III in 1267 and as such he came to court as the Prince of Wales. However, his relationship with Henry's successor, Edward I, was not a good one and Welsh and English interests were often at odds. This resulted in Welsh resistance, invasion by Edward I and Llewelyn's death in December 1282.

A courting couple, Valerie Lee and Malcolm Beames, seated in Crown Gardens, which was later to become the site of the Welsh Office's car park, c. 1952. Park Place can be seen in the background.

The South African War Memorial, the work of Albert Toft, was erected in memory of around 200 soldiers who were killed serving in Welsh regiments. One of the most notable of these occasions was the battle of Rorke's Drift, the 120th anniversary of which was celebrated on 22 January 1999. This was a famous battle in which eleven Victoria Crosses were won – the highest number ever awarded for a single battle. One hundred and twenty soldiers held off some 4,000 Zulu warriors.

The University of Wales opened its west wing in 1909. The remainder of the building was completed between 1912 and 1962. It is now the main building of Cardiff University, containing the school of Biosciences, the department of Chemistry, and the department of Earth Sciences.

UNIVERSITY COLLEGE, CARDIFF.

The interior of drapers' library, at the University of Wales, c. 1937.

The National Museum of Wales, c. 1927. To the right of the picture is the equine statue of Godfrey Charles Morgan, the First Viscount Lord Tredegar, mounted on his Balaclava charger, Sir Briggs erected in 1909.

This statue of John Cory the coal owner and philanthropist was erected outside the City Hall in 1906.

This statute by T.J. Clapperton is in the Marble Hall and depicts Esgob Morgan – Bishop Morgan, who died in 1604. 'Morgan's translation of the Bible into Welsh, published in 1588, was a great literary achievement' – J. Glyn Davies.

A representation of Sir Thomas Picton (1758-1815) in the Marble Hall, carved by T. Menburn Crook RBS. Picton was Wellington's chief lieutenant in the Peninsular War and the Waterloo Campaign (18 June 1815) and it was here that he met his end, when a musket ball struck his head. It was later discovered that he had concealed a wound to his hip, received a few days earlier, which must have pained him greatly.

The foundation stone of the National Museum of Wales was laid in 1912, but owing to the intervention of the First World War the main block and western galleries were not completed and opened until 1927.

The Marble Hall offers a 'hall of fame' showing Cardiffians their history. This statue of Dafydd Ab Gwilym, a fourteenth-century poet, sculpted by W.W. Wagstaff is one of them. With the conquest of Wales by Edward I in the thirteenth century, Wales' bardic tradition was almost eradicated; but Dafydd, now considered to be one of the great poets in medieval Europe, instigated a revival in the fourteenth century using a flexible verse form called 'cywydd'. 'The Welsh romantic is represented as a gentle bard. He carries a harp and looks as though he is about to burst forth into song' – *Welsh Historical Sculpture* catalogue, 1916.

A sculpture by Henry Pool RBS of Giraldus Cambrensis – Gerald of Wales, or to use his Norman name 'Gerald De Barri' (1146-1223). Gerald was born in Pembrokeshire, studied in Paris and is considered one of the greatest Welsh writers in Latin. He travelled extensively and his observations on his beloved Wales, most notably in his *Itinerarium Kambriae* and *Descriptio Kambriae* brought the country to the world's notice. 'He began life as an aristocratic Norman and ended a Welsh patriot.' – W. Llewellyn Williams KC, MP.

Many Cardiffians will remember the circle in front of the City Hall with its stone pillars and iron chains as seen here, c. 1960.

The Marble Hall contains figures from all periods of history, and includes Buddug – Boadicea, who died AD 61. The sculptor was Professor J. Havard Thomas. Boadicea was the wife of Prastagus, King of the Iceni, a tribe of Ancient Britains. She is often cited as the most powerful historical Celtic female figure and the one who led southern Britain in insurrection against the Romans.

Finally from the Marble Hall, Dewi Sant – Saint David, the sixth-century patron saint of Wales. It was sculpted by Sir William Goscombe John RA. This most famous and well-loved patron of Wales was a Celtic monk, abbot and bishop and during his life, was the archbishop of Wales. He was one of many early saints who helped to spread Christianity among the pagan Celtic tribes of western Britain.

Two
Streets and Buildings

High Street, Cardiff

The High Street in Cardiff in 1928. The entrance to Cardiff Castle can be seen in the centre and there is a Rolls Royce parked on the extreme right.

St Mary Street with James Howell & Co. to the right, *c.* 1923. The entrance to the Central Market is just under H. Samuel's clock in the centre. The Castle can be seen through the High Street.

St Mary Street, *c.* 1912. Note the awnings on the shops along the right hand side of the street. These were more important in the days when produce was displayed outside and before refrigeration. They also provided a convenient advertising space.

St Mary Street, *c.* 1904. St Mary Street was originally named after St Mary's church which was washed away in the great flood of 1607.

St Mary Street in 1909. 'Once upon a time St Mary Street was made up of town houses of the local gentry. Lewis of the Van, Mathews of Llandaff, Basset of Beau Pre, each had their town residence to which they would come during the winter months' – *Cardiff: Notes Picturesque and Biographical* by J. Kyrle Fletcher.

St Mary Street, *c.* 1904. The sign to the right of the handcart points to the Bethany Baptist chapel which used to be in Wharton Street.

St Mary Street, *c.* 1904. The name is said to have come into being in the first half of the sixteenth century after the division of Cardiff into two parishes. The church is said to date from the eleventh century.

Queen Street, c. 1906. The Empire Theatre, on the left, opened in 1887 as Levino's Hall and later became the Gaumont Cinema. It is now a C&A department store.

Queen Street, c. 1929. This view was taken from a little further down Queen Street than the one above and the Empire Theatre, on the extreme left, can be seen more clearly. Note also, the ornate tram wires with street lighting running down the centre of the road.

Queen Street, *c*. 1929. 'Queen Street is a modern name given to an old street in honour of Queen Victoria, but I like its old name better – Crockherbtown' – *Cardiff: Notes Picturesque and Biographical* by J. Kyrle Fletcher.

Queen Street, 1909. The Tivoli Hotel, to the right, was established at 30 Queen Street in 1909. It was demolished in 1978.

Queen Street in the early twentieth century. The Victoria Hotel at 44 Queen Street, to the extreme right, dates back to 1897.

Queen Street, *c.* 1904. 'Remember me to all at Ardwyn', wrote Walter L. Talbot when he sent this postcard to Miss A. Pratt of Fleet Street, Torquay, on 13 August 1904.

Queen Street in 1904. This appears to be a posed shot, with a double decked and single decked tram halted while the tram driver and a policeman stand to attention.

Park Hall Buildings, Queen Street. The Park Hotel, on the right, was built in the French renaissance style in 1885.

Queen Street, *c.* 1910. Once known as Crockherbtown, it was renamed Queen Street in honour of Queen Victoria by resolution of the town council in December 1886.

Queen Street, *c.* 1903. The popular Dutch Café is to the extreme left.

Queen Street, *c.* 1908. In 1853 an unsuccessful attempt was made to change the name Queen Street to Park Street.

Queen Street in the mid-1950s. Trolleybuses had now taken over from trams and the ornate tram wires, which had been in the centre of the road, had been replaced by more functional poles on each side of the road. The vehicle, near left, was used for the maintenance of overhead wires used by the trams and trolleybuses.

Dolcis shoe stores in the 1970s. This shop (seen centre left in the previous picture), was in the process of being redeveloped and as so often happened, this was achieved by demolishing the back portion of the building, leaving the frontage intact.

An aerial view, showing Queen Street running left to right in the foreground in the 1970s. Mackcross stores (centre) is to the left of Dolcis shoe stores; the distinctive frontage can be recognized from the previous picture. In the background is Penarth point, overlooking the sea.

The changing face of Queen Street. Of these five businesses in Queen Street only the Midland Bank, to the right, remains today, and this will soon change its name to HSBC.

A busy Queen Street, *c.* 1970. This shows the pedestrianized junction of Queen Street and Paradise Place.

The Taff Vale pub on the corner of Queen Street and Paradise Place, a few years earlier than the previous picture. This gives a clearer view of this corner building, no longer a pub by 1978, with its side door entrance in Paradise Place. It also shows a time when cars could drive in the central areas of Cardiff, before pedestrianization.

Further down Paradise Place in 1974. The Cardiff Comrades club, to the right, is where Shirley Bassey had her 'big break' in show business. Agent, Georgie Wood was so impressed with her performance, he booked her to appear on the *Memories of Jolson* show.

The following sequence of photographs show the Ebenezer church in Ebenezer Street at the end of Paradise Place which was opened on 3 December 1828.

The Ebenezer church in 1974. It was originally built in the 1820s at a cost of £850, but by the '70s it was in a dilapidated state as can be seen above. Below is the chapel organ.

Two interior views of the Ebenezer church taken before it was demolished in 1974. The view above looks towards the back of the church, showing the upstairs pews. Below, the front of the church can be seen, including three memorial plaques, the steps up to the pulpit and part of the organ.

Private chambers in Ebenezer church, 5 February 1974. The painting above the antique fireplace is believed to be that of the Revd Lewis Powell.

The vestry in 1974. Beyond the main body of the church were private rooms; on the wall can be seen mounted photographs of church members.

The corner of Ebenezer Street and Paradise Place, *c.* 1970. The high-rise Pearl Assurance building is in the background.

Frederick Street looking towards Queen Street, *c.* 1977. The Pearl Assurance building is once again visible. In ancient days a market was held in this street.

Hills Terrace, *c.* 1977. The rear of Mackcross building can be seen in the centre.

An aerial view of the central area of Cardiff, in the 1970s. In the centre is St Johns church and in the top right the famous Cardiff Arms Park, which was demolished in 1998, can be seen.

The rear of Charles Street in the 1970s. The Grass Roots Coffee Bar is to the left.

The back of terraced cottages in Charles Street, *c.* 1966. St David's Cathedral can be seen to the right.

The site of the extension for Littlewoods in Charles Street which was built in the late 1960s. It involved major construction, with deep foundation digging, the beginning of which can be seen below. The extension was officially opened in 1970 but the store closed in 1998.

Workmen laying the foundations of the Littlewoods extension building. The site was taken over by Marks and Spencer in 1998.

When the houses in Little Union Street were demolished, Marks and Spencer used the site to build a car park.

CITY OF CARDIFF.

Freehold Corner Business Premises,
St. John's Square & Queen Street.

Plans, Particulars & Conditions of Sale

OF

——VALUABLE——

FREEHOLD BUSINESS PREMISES

SITUATE AND BEING

No. 2, Queen Street,

—— AND ——

No. 1, St. John's Square,

CARDIFF,

Now in the occupation of Messrs. Masters & Company and their undertenants, and which will be offered for

SALE BY AUCTION

AT THE MART, 5, HIGH STREET, CARDIFF,

On THURSDAY, the 14th day of MAY, 1908,

At 3 o'clock in the Afternoon, by

Messrs.

Stephenson & Alexander.

Plans, Particulars and Conditions of Sale may be obtained upon application to Messrs. VAUGHAN and ROCHE, Solicitors, Bute Docks, Cardiff, or to the Auctioneers, 5, High Street, Cardiff.

Stephenson & Alexander (S&A), Industrial and Commercial Surveyors, have been in professional practice for more than 160 years and still operate from 5 High Street. This advertises the sale of a prime city centre site by Messrs Masters & Company. (See the map on p. 6 for the precise location.)

PREMISES FOR SALE

The 'premises for sale' on the junction of Queen Street, St John's Square, Duke Street and North Road (now Kingsway) in 1908. This was, and is, a prime site and the annual rent for the property shown was £350. To quote from the sales information, 'The Auctioneers desire to call the attention of Capitalists and others to this important Sale, as it is daily becoming more difficult to obtain a Freehold Property anywhere in the business centre of the City, the demand for such Properties at the moment considerably exceeding the supply.'

Free Library, Cardiff

The Free Library in The Hayes in the early years of the twentieth century. The central library in Trinity Street owed its beginnings to Mr Peter Price a local architect who made several attempts to implement the adoption of the Public Libraries Acts, 1850-1855. When the acts were implemented in 1862, the entire contents of a voluntary library in St Mary Street were handed over to the corporation. Cardiff was the first local authority in Wales to adopt the Acts and provide a public library. This building in The Hayes was opened in 1882 and forms the northern end; the southern end was completed in 1896 and was opened by the Prince of Wales, later King Edward VII. John Ballinger, whose statue can be seen above, was appointed librarian in 1884. He resigned as chief librarian in 1908 when he took the post of chief librarian at the National Library of Wales at Aberystwyth. For more than 100 years the old library served Cardiffians well and many people will have fond memories of it.

Below opposite: Duke Street, *c.* 1920. Cardiff Tramways purchased a prototype double decked, covered top tram in 1923 which seated sixty-four people. A further eighty trams of similar style were purchased over the next two years. Between 1536 and 1810 this road was known as Shoemaker Street. It was widened in 1924 when the row of shops abutting on the castle wall was demolished. Originally called Duckstrete, the name suggests an association with poulterer's shops. However, some romantics say it owes its name to the sojourn of the Duke of Normandy in Cardiff Castle for more than twenty-five years.

Looking down towards the main entrance of the library, *c.* 1980. Over the years thousands of people climbed these stairs to the reference library. Note the ornate lighting on the pedestal at the end of the stairs, and the dual language map of Cardiff on the wall.

The music department on the ground floor. The three library assistants to the right are, left to right: Val Parker Jean Collins and Spencer Basford.

The committee room on the first floor, c. 1980. This room was originally used for meetings of the library committee. It was also used, in later years, for staff interviews and meetings.

The research room on the second floor. The busts are of Marcus Gunn (sculpted in dark stone) and William Saunders. Both were strong supporters of the Central Library from its beginning.

The ground floor lending library, *c.* 1980. Library assistant Jenny Fenn is seated on the right.

The main reference library where Cardiff author, Jack Jones, researched his novels about Cardiff and the valleys, *c.* 1980. Note the high ceilings with decorated coving; however, signs of dilapidation are beginning to show on the ceiling.

A plaque to 'Colonel Bertram Jarvis'. This plaque in the old library depicts 'Colonel' Bertram Jarvis a well-known sandwich board man who walked the streets of Cardiff for more than thirty years. In 1939 his photograph appeared in the famous *Picture Post* magazine advertising the Embassy Skating Ring that used to be in Cathays Terrace.

A plaque to T.E. Lawrence (1888-1935), 'Lawrence of Arabia'. He was born in Tremadic, Caernarvon, and his Welsh background proved to be beneficial when at Jesus College, Oxford. He refused the Victoria Cross and turned down a knighthood.

A plaque to John Ballinger, librarian at Cardiff library from 1884 to 1908, which says, 'This tablet was placed here by his many friends to commemorate his great services to the Cardiff Library and to Literature and Education in Wales.'

Behind the scenes in the library, April 1986. All the bookbinding took place in the main workroom; note the finished bound copies (left), unbound copies, stitched ready for their covers (next to them) and the press used to finish the process (right). Note also the pot of glue, with brush, in the foreground. The date was identified from the calendar with the help of a magnifying glass!

Hone & Jones Ltd, house furnishing, was situated at 28 Bridge Street in the 1950s.

Wood Street in the early 1970s. The Wood Street Congregational church can be seen to the right which was at one time used as a theatre.

An advertising hoarding outside Cardiff general railway station, c. 1979.

The Wales Empire Swimming Pool in the 1970s. Built by Cardiff Corporation with the 1958 Empire and Commonwealth Games in mind (and to provide Cardiffians with a modern swimming baths) this venue was sadly demolished in 1998 to make way for the new rugby stadium. The pool proved popular with international swimmers and ordinary people alike. During its short life of forty years, thousands of people took advantage of the pool's many facilities and people would travel from all parts of the country to visit there. The pool was 55yds long by 20yds wide shelving in depth from 3ft to 16ft. It was, at the time, the most modern swimming pool in Britain with a first class restaurant, aeratone therapeutic bath, hot showers room, Turkish baths, physiotherapy rooms and so forth. The 1,722 permanent tip-up seats were supplemented by around 750 temporary seats.

Below opposite: The Pavilion in Sophia Gardens was built for the 1951 Festival of Britain and was the venue for concerts, boxing, wrestling, dances and exhibitions until its roof caved in after heavy snow in 1981.

The original swimming pool reception area, c. 1960.

The teaching pool was opened by the Lord Mayor of Cardiff, the Rt Hon. Alderman Winifred Mathias on 18 April 1973. She is seen here receiving flowers from a gold swimming award winner.

Schoolchildren learning to swim in the teaching pool, under the watchful eyes of an instructor and observed by Alderman Winifred Mathias on 18 April 1973.

The diving springboards were of the latest design with both fibreglass and aluminium types available. The highest was a solid diving board.

The boiler house, c. 1987. Each oil-fired boiler had a capacity of 5,000lbs of steam per hour and provided steam for all the services in the building.

The pool filtering plant, c. 1960. Some 636,000 gallons of water filled the pool and was circulated continuously by pumps; thus a constant supply of filtered and chlorinated water was distributed around the pool.

The pool's hydro spin-dryer, c. 1960. The restaurant was capable of accommodating 156 diners and these machines were used to wash and dry the many tablecloths, tea towels, staff uniforms and Turkish bath towels that were used daily.

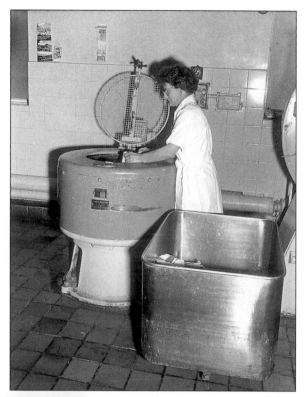

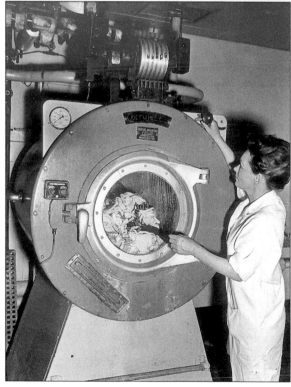

The pool's washing machine. This Corrujet 65 model was made by Thomas Bradford & Co., Manchester.

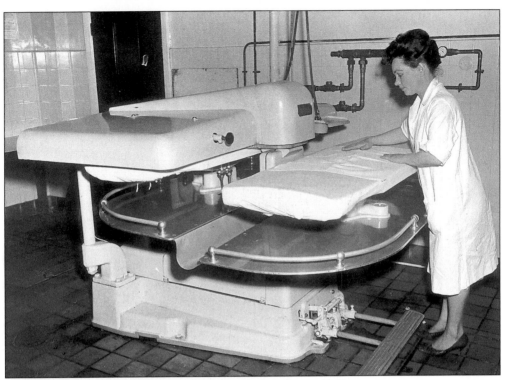

One of the twin rapid presses in use in the pool's laundry, c. 1960.

After an aeratone therapeutic bath, facilities were provided for a restful half-hour, c. 1960.

In 1970 the length of the pool had to be shortened to meet international standards.

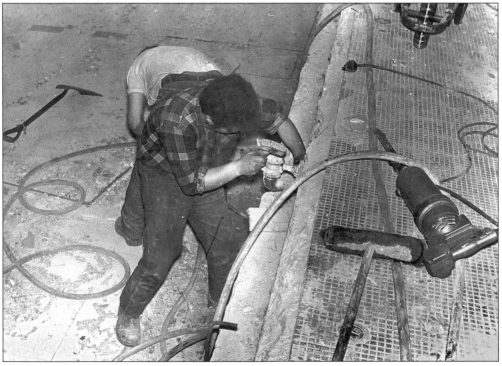

The pool was shortened from 55yds to 50 metres.

Adam Street in the 1970s. The area has greatly changed since this picture was taken. The wall to the right is part of Cardiff prison.

The new Fire Service headquarters and central fire station was opened on 30 March 1973 in Adam Street after some of these buildings had been demolished.

Newport Road in February 1967. There is a striking difference between the Georgian terraces on the left had side of the street and the more recent high-rise buildings on the right.

The University College of South Wales and Monmouthshire opened in 1883 at Newport Road in the old Cardiff Infirmary building. These two photographs show the college sometime in the early years of the century.

The Julian Hodge Building,
Newport Road, c. 1967. The
building houses Chartered Trust
plc and ACL Life.

Churchill Way in the late
1970s. It was once known as
Pembroke Terrace and the
dock's feeder ran along it. Some
people confuse the Glamorgan
Canal with the docks feeder
channel which was cut around
1836 as a means of feeding the
Bute West Dock.

The rear of Nos 33, 34, and 35 Love Lane. In 1955 Wilfred Sullivan lived at 33, Patrick Regan at 34 and Jeremiah Fitzgerald at 35. The ramshackle building on the right is an outside lavatory.

Love Lane was situated off Little Frederick Street. It was said to mark the site of a plot of land known as Tri-chwarter Caerdydd in 1764.

Three

Shops and
Businesses

Huxleys Medical Stores on Bridge Street, c. 1955.

Fry's Darts in Bridge Street, *c.* 1978. The store catered for the needs of indoor sportsmen and women.

The Queen's Head pub at 34 Bridge Street. It was established in 1858.

Owens the gents' hairdressers (centre left) on the corner of Union Street and Bridge Street, *c.* 1955. To the far left is the Queen's Head public house and a few doors down the street, to the right, is Huxley's chemist.

The junction of Union Street and Bridge Street, *c.* 1955. The Queen's Head pub can be seen more clearly on the left, with a sign advertising Rhumney beers.

The rear of Rapport & Co. Ltd wholesalers in Millicent Street (right), *c.* 1955.

Little Frederick Street, *c.* 1955. The van on the right is parked outside the Taff Garage Company.

Bradshaw Bush newsagents and tobacconist traded at 45 Tredegar Street, c. 1954. Cigarette advertising covered a large part of the hoarding area, including, Players, Park Drive and Woodbines.

The Hayes Bookshop, purveyor of antiquarian books, on the corner of Hayes Bridge Road and Bridge Street, c. 1970.

John Bull (Jaybee Ltd) grocery stores, on the junction of Bridge Street and Hayes Bridge Road, c. 1955.

Christopher Irwin, the first manager of the Electricity Board showrooms. The shop opened on The Hayes just before the Second World War. Mr Irwin is seen here sitting in front of an electric fire display. Mr Irwin died during the war.

The interior of the Electricity Board showrooms in the 1930s. The building which the showrooms occupied was once used by a fish market and, much later in 1998, Habitat took over the building.

The Hayes at the turn of the century. The tall building on the left is the extension to David Morgan (built in 1884), next, in order, is David Morgan's original shop, then the Duke of Cornwall public house, the 1893 extension to David Morgan and, finally, the Royal George public house.

Lovell & Christmas (Liverpool) Ltd, situated in New Street next to Dowdall O'Mahoney, *c*. 1955.

Mill Lane Market, *c*. 1955. The first floor of the building in the centre was occupied by Tripple-Tex Tailoring. The lower storey was occupied by a variety of shops including a florist and, at the right end, a public convenience.

Coopers Snack Bar on Mill Lane, c. 1955. The Fruit Exchange and Richard England buildings are in the background.

L. Weisbard & Son, woodworkers supplies, on the corner of Frederick Street and Canal Street, c. 1976.

Canada House occupied a site almost opposite L.Weisbard & Son. During the Blitz the residents of Frederick Street took shelter there when the air-raid siren sounded.

John Blagden, chief projectionist at the Odeon Cinema in Queen Street. He worked for the Rank Organisation for more than fifty years.

All the people in this picture, believed to have been taken at the Capitol Cinema in Queen Street in 1968, were members of The Rank Organisation 25 Year Club, having worked for the company for at least that number of years. Mr Blagden can be seen fifth from the left second row from the back.

In the 1930s Frederick Beames ran a well-known taxi service called Beamestax which ran all around the city. His wife, Beatrice, and Mrs Emily Buck pose in front of one of the Beamestax saloon cars, c. 1930.

The frontage of T.P. Martin, 9 Castle Street, chemist and photographer, in the Coronation year, 1953. The shop closed in 1966.

Morgan Edwards, The Heating Centre and J. Phillips the Gentlemen's Hairdressers in Castle Street, *c.* 1960. The office space above the shops was 'To Let'.

Coach and horses were still in vogue when this picture was taken outside James Howell's in St Mary Street before the First World War. The Borough Arms, also known as the Bodega at one time, is to the left.

Anthonie, the gown shop, in High Street in the 1970s. The premises were up for sale when this picture was taken.

Olivers shoe shop on the corner of Church Street and High Street. Olivers occupied this building for many years, but in 1997 it became a showroom for kitchens.

Courts furnishing store on High Street, c. 1970. The store is now based in Newport Road.

The offices of *The Western Mail* and *South Wales News*, on St Mary Street opposite Wharton Street, *c*. 1930. The *South Wales News* later became the *South Wales Echo*. The building was called Golate House and Golate Lane is to the right.

David Evans (right) serves tea to fellow *South Wales Echo* process room workers Harry Ferris (left) and Bill Webber, *c*. 1932.

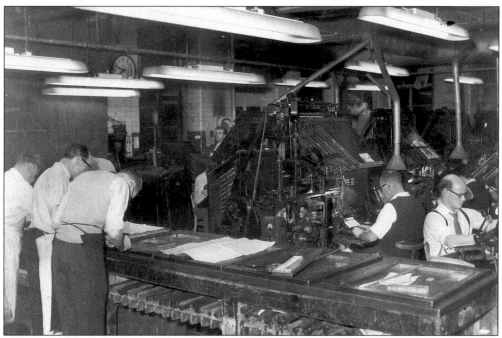

Western Mail & Echo composing room in the St Mary Street office. Left to right: Idwal Morgan, George Murphy and Cliff Davies are bent over 'the stone' and Reg Rees (first right) and Jack Chamberlain are seated at their linotype machines, *c*. 1957.

The composing room at Thomson House, Havelock Street, on the occasion of the retirement of composing room overseer George Codd in 1971. The offices had moved to Havelock Street in 1961.

Composing room apprentices, 1962. They are, left to right: Glyn Coward, David Adams (in front), Andrew Smith, Bob Tyler, Ralph Snook, Gilbert Davies, Mike O'Leary, David Gordon-Roberts, Derek Hoare.

South Wales Echo maintenance team, *c*. 1980. They are, left to right, back row: Bob Keeble, Ben Davies, Paul Tyler, John Norman, David Ellis. Front row: Phil Sparkes, Roy Strong.

The retirement celebrations of Ted Perriam, of the *Western Mail* machine room, in 1966. Among those pictured are: John Baldwin, Peter Clifton, Mac Beames, Arthur Parry, John Haines, Bob Potter, John Sweeney, Ken Miles, David Jones, Bert Oakey, Lennie Johnson.

The retirement of Harry Ferris, process room manager (centre right). He is seen here shaking hands with Jack Phillips. On the extreme left is John Sweeney, the stereo department overseer. On the extreme right is his wife, Ann. Harry Ferris retired in the first week of January 1979, after fifty-one years with the paper.

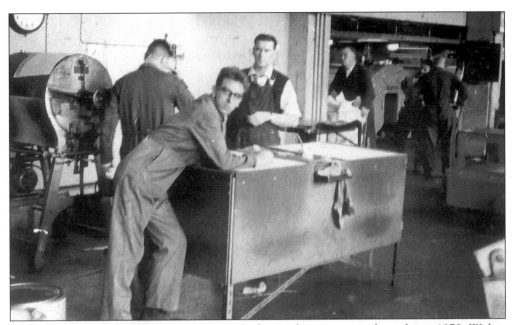

Western Mail & Echo stereo department with the machine room to the right, *c.* 1970. Walter Hopwood, with his back to the camera, is drying the paper mâché matrix in the gas dryer. Brian Lee (the author) is seen leaning on the packing table with Reg Potter to his right.

Western Mail & Echo stereo department, Thomson House, Havelock Street, *c.* 1970. John Haines (centre) examines the hot metal rotary plate which has just been cast and Reg Potter, to the left with chisel in hand, is about to trim the plate. Looking on is a hostess from the television show *Double Your Money*, who was probably appearing that week at the New Theatre.

The retirement celebrations of stereotyper Bert James in 1973. They are, left to right, at the back: Silas Wilson, Eric Stoker, Ken Miles, Bill Marks (obscured), Reg Potter, Stan Parsons, Bob Potter, Lennie Johnson, John English, John Norman, Ralph Frost (works manager). At the front: Brian Lee, Bert James, Walter Hopwood.

David Thomas (fourth left), managing director of *Western Mail & Echo*, is seen here presenting gold watches to staff with forty years service in 1969. Among them were Harry Collins, Hector Collins, George Codd, Trevor Jones and on the extreme right William 'Billy' Lee.

Western Mail & Echo staff posing for a picture before setting off to Bath Races in 1972.

Western Mail & Echo carpenter Charles Bidlecombe receiving a cheque from company secretary Philip Leader on the occasion of his retirement in 1979.

Accounts department staff at the *Western Mail & Echo* in 1973. The man in the middle is Malcolm Perrins.

Machine room overseer Dennis Donovan's retirement in 1980. He is fourth from the left on the front row. The only one with a drink in his hand is Geoff Rich (extreme right) the Echo's editor!

Four

Sport

Members of the 1954 Wales team pose at the City Hall before flying to Vancouver for the Empire and Commonwealth Games.

Cardiff boxer Malcolm Collins carrying the Welsh flag at the Empire and Commonwealth Games in 1958. The Empire and Commonwealth Games came to Cardiff in this year.

The flags of the Commonwealth at the Cardiff Arms Park which staged the track and field events.

A track event in progress. In the background can be seen the Post Office telephone building in Park Street.

The Australian, Dave Power, after winning the 6 miles track event on 19 July. He later went on to win the gruelling marathon race on 24 July, establishing a new Games best performance of 2 hrs, 22 mins, 45.6 secs.

Athletes running away from the camera (!) towards Westgate Street. The officials (in white trousers, dark blazers and light Panama hats) can be seen in the central area.

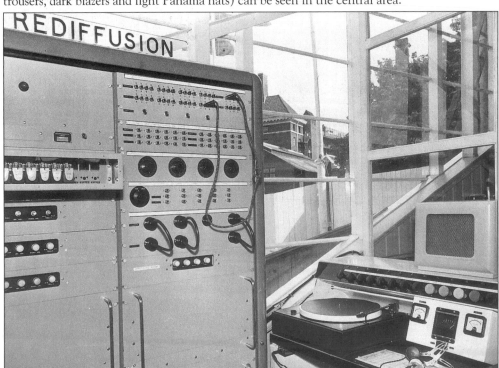

The Queen's speech, on the final day, was relayed to the spectators from this room after being taped by the BBC in London. The speech contained the proclamation of Prince Charles as Prince of Wales.

Eddie Williams posing with his prizes around 1900. He was awarded the Mayor of Cardiff's prize at a Sophia Gardens sports meeting on 8 September 1900 and went on to win the world famous Welsh Powderhall Handicap Sprint at Taff Vale Park, Pontypridd, in 1921.

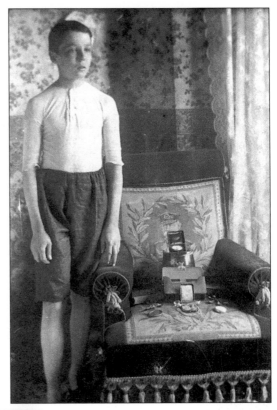

A signed portrait of Eddie Williams, Welsh Powderhall winner, in 1921.

Roath (Cardiff) Harriers cross-country team, 1966. The officials are: Ted Hopkins (right, middle row),Viv Pitcher (second right, middle row), Bob Tawton (right, second row), Ken Harris (second right, front row). Among the runners are: Brian Griffiths, Bill Pryce, Norman John, Cecil Oakley, John Walsh, Jeff Kirby, Dilwyn Reynolds, Steve Prichard, Brian Lee, Mac Beames (with his son, Nicholas).

Brian Lee (extreme right) gets the *Western Mail & Echo* team off to a good start in the 1982 Cardiff Business House Relays at Pontcanna Recreation Fields.

The Cardiff Business House relay team winners in 1982. They are, left to right: Malcolm Farnham, Brian Lee, Rodney Savage, Lee Beames.

British heavyweight boxing champion, Jack Peterson (third left), towers over this group of sporting gentlemen at Cardiff in the 1930s.

An army boxing team *en route* to a meeting. Joe Erskine, Dai Dower and Malcolm Collins are just three of the well-known Welsh boxers who competed for the army in the early 1950s.

Malcolm Collins, one of Wales's greatest amateur boxers, dubbed 'The Welsh Walloper'. Not many of his opponents lasted more than one round. Note the Prince of Wales crest on his vest.

A Wales *v.* The Army match at Sophia Gardens Pavilion in 1954. Collins (left) has Gordon Blakey, whom he beat, on the canvas.

Malcolm Collins scoring a great victory over the famed Scotsman Dick McTaggart at Sophia Gardens Pavilion in 1954.

'South Paw' Malcolm Collins pushes down a left from G.J. Coetzee (South Africa) in their semi-final match at the Empire Games boxing championships at Sophia Gardens Pavilion. Collins went on to take his second silver medal, but some boxing critics thought he should have been awarded the gold.

Malcolm Collins raises his hand in victory after his defeat of New Zealander M.S. Purton in the quarter-finals at the 1958 Empire and Commonwealth Games.

Malcolm Collins British Featherweight Champion, 1957/8. He shows off his championship cups and international representative plaques and is wearing the 1958 Empire and Commonwealth Games blazer.

Pontcanna Albions AFC in 1922. Sadly, the names of these players are not known.

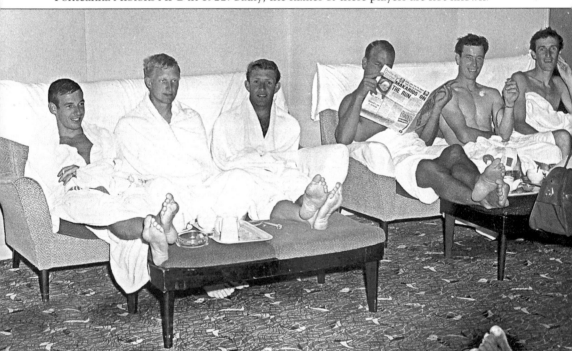

Cardiff City and Wales soccer players enjoying a break after a training session at the Empire Swimming Pool, *c.* 1960. They are, left to right: Barrie Hole, Trevor Peck, Steve Gammon, John Charles, Derek Tapscott, Sandy Milneu.

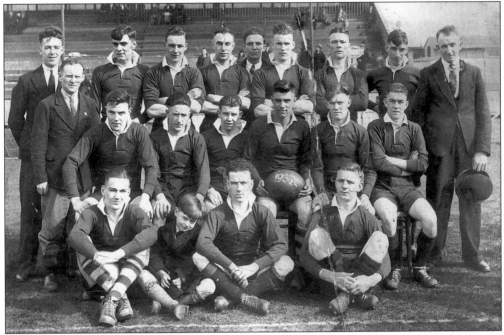

The *Western Mail & Echo* rugby team in front of the old Ely Racecourse grandstand in 1932. Among the players are: Chris Godwin (holding the ball), Albert Godwin, Dennis Donovan, Jack Phillips, Albert Johnson, Tommy Andrews.

Cardiff RFC staged the formal opening of the magnificent Gwyn Nicholls Memorial Gates at the Arms Park on Boxing Day 1949. The ceremony was performed by Rhys T. Gabe, a lifelong friend of, and co-centre, with Gwyn Nicholls.

The Prince of Wales on a visit to the famous Arms Park to watch an international rugby match in 1969. He is seen here accompanied by WRU president, Ivor Jones. By the end of eighty minutes Wales had beaten Ireland, 24-11.

A Royal Visit in 1980. The Queen and Duke of Edinburgh visited the Arms Park to see a rugby match between a combined England and Wales team against a combined Scotland and Ireland team. The former team won 37-33. The match was played in the centenary year of the Welsh Rugby Union of which the Queen is patron.

Cardiff's famed lineout jumper Robert Norster in action at the Arms Park during the 1988 Wales *v.* France rugby international match.

Neil Kinnock, leader of the parliamentary Labour Party (1983-1992), was at the Arms Park in 1990 and is seen here applauding a neat piece of play.

Peter Walker batting for Glamorgan against the Australians in 1961.

Yorkshire's Geoff Boycott lets a delivery from Peter Swart through to wicket keeper Eifion Jones at Sophia Gardens in 1979.

Cardiff Arms Park by night in 1977. The Arms Park had many uses and hosted many events. The occasion seen here is a greyhound racing meeting.

Cardiff Arms Park Greyhounds final racecard. The last meeting took place on 30 July 1977. Mr M. Davies's 'Lillyput Queen' won the last race to be held at the world famous rugby venue.

8th Race — 484m Flat — 9·00p.m.

1st £25 .... 2nd £4 .... Others £2 .... TIME..................

PLOVER MIKE
W/F.D. Ploverfield King — O – MR. H.W. LODGE
Jan'74 Quick Jane — T – F. McCARTHY

Jy 25	484m	G	T1	3	1¼	Tonyrefail	30.60 Hin 1.	27.8	5/1	30.74
Jy 23	484m	G	T2	2	5	Lovely Excuse	30.63 CR	28.2	5/2	31.03
Jy 16	484m	G	T2	5	7	Alley's Pendel	30.34 Hin St. RO ½. Ch 3.	27.6	7/1	30.91

CLIFFS STORY
W/F.D. Camira Story — O – MR. J. LYNCH
Feb'75. Freedom Lady — T – P. DOYLE

Jy 23	484m	G	T2	5	8¼	Alley's Pendel	30.40 SA. Hin 1.	29.5	10/1	31.05
Jy 18	484m	G	T3	1	3	Lillyput Queen	30.33 FA. Ld RU.	28.8	7/1	30.33
Jy 16	484m	G	T3	1	¼	Feagh Destiny	30.78 FA. Ld ¼.	29.0	2/1JF	30.78

POSTMAN JIM
Bd.D. Gypsy Jim — O – MRS. S. V. QUINN
June'74 Geraldines Ivy — T – MRS.O.M.BARRY

Jy 23	484m	G	T6	1	6	Primrose Boy	30.47 FA. AL. Hin 1.	29.5	7/2	30.47
Jy 16	484m	G	T4	4	3	Cliff's Story	30.78 SA.	29.5	5/1	31.02
Jy 9	647m	G	T6	5	15½	Orjay	41.80 FA. CR.	29.6	7/1	43.04
Jy 6	647m	G	T4				42.40 SA.	29.5	ST	42.40
Jy 4	484m	F	T4	4	3	Sonny	31.21 FA. Bpd 1.	29.7	7/2	31.45

LILLYPUT QUEEN
W.Bk.B. Sole Aim — O – MR. M. DAVIES.
April'75 Quann's Queen — T – F. GOODMAN
(CARDIFF)
S. 1.5.77.

Jy 25	484m	G	T6	4	10½	Kensington Queen	29.96 FA. Bpd 1.	26.5	7/1	30.80
Jy 18	484m	G	T4	2	3	Cliff's Story	30.33 FA. CR.	26.5	7/2	30.57
Jy 13	484m	G	T6				30.98	26.7	ST	30.98
Jy 6	277m	G	T6	1	3	Ballykilty Rover	17.33 FA. AL.	26.4	Tr2	17.33

BRIGHT FELLOW
Bd.D. Bright Lad — O – MR. M. DAVIES
Oct'74 Proud Joan — T – R. LANGDON

Jy 25	484m	G	T6	1	SHd	Lovely Excuse	30.59 FA. Ld RU	36.4	5/4 F	30.59
Jy 18	484m	G	T5	3	3½	Cliffs Story	30.33 (W) 1 RO ½	36.5	6/1	30.60
Jy 11	484m	G	T5	1	1¼	Dunmain Tara	30.93 Hin ¼(W).RO ½.Ld ¼.	36.2	3/1	30.93

LOVELY EXCUSE
Bk.D. Monalee Champion — O – MR. D. ALLEN
Jne'75 Unbeaten Record — T – P. DOYLE

Jy 25	484m	G	T4	2	SHd	Bright Fellow	30.59 FA (W) ¼. RO. SF.	32.0	9/4	30.60
Jy 23	484m	G	T4	1	5	Plover Mike	30.63 CR(W)RO ½ Ld 3	32.0	5/4F	30.63
Jy 16	470m	S1	T5	5	10¼	Rathduff Spring	29.10 (Bristol)	31.6	33/1	29.53
Ju 27	484m	G	T5	1	2¼	Ballyrane Lad	30.78 CR.	31.5	7/1	30.78

Whippet racing, which was popular in Wales in the 1920s and '30s, is slowly coming back into vogue. However, there are no £1,000 prizes on offer these days!

Five
Events

An artists impression of the entrance to the Cardiff Fine Art, Industrial and Maritime Exhibition of 1896, which was situated in Park Place, Cathays Park.

The exhibition buildings in Cathays Park, 1896. It was held here for five months and attracted around a million visitors from all parts of the country.

PC Alfred Rich, seen here standing on the bank of the River Taff, was based at B Division, Canton police station, in 1896. He was a regular visitor to the exhibition in his role as a police officer.

The exhibition had its own railway station and trains brought thousands of visitors from the valleys.

BUFFALO BILL'S WILD WEST

The official programme for Buffalo Bill's Wild West show which came to Cardiff in 1891, 1903 and 1904.

Buffalo Bill Cody with Chief Sitting Bull around the turn of the century. The caption to this newspaper picture reads 'Sitting Bull and Buffalo Bill. Foes in '76—Friends in '85'. Buffalo Bill died penniless in 1917.

The native Americans, then known as Red Indians, set up their village of teepees and tents on the bank of the River Taff in Sophia Gardens.

112

A page from the official programme for the Wild West Show. A record crowd of 22,000 people packed Sophia Gardens in 1903 to see Sioux, Arraphoe, Brule and Cheyenne tribes in full war paint.

Cathedral Road Sunday school's Band of Hope around the turn of the century. The white banners read 'Less Pubs, Less Prisons, Less Prisoners, Less Rates' and 'Reductions of Facilities means Reduction of Crime'.

Cathedral Road Sunday school Band of Hope. The signs on the side of the carriage reads, 'The children cry pass the bill, less pubs the children's inheritance.'

This picture, taken around the time of the previous two photographs, is thought to be a 'Lifeboat Saturday' fund-raising event.

Westgate Street post office telegram boys' band on 25 May 1901. Fifth from the left on the second row is David Thomas Morgan who was popularly known as 'Tom'.

Soldiers marching from Maindy Barracks to the Great Western railway station at the start of the First World War. People lined the streets to give their men a good send off.

Off to foreign fields. The platform at the Great Western railway station was crowded with relatives waving off their loved ones.

The Soldiers Rest was situated above the Wyndham Arcade in St Mary Street.

City of Cardiff RAF Cadets Squadron 1344 in March 1943.

A Boys Brigade Guard of Honour in the civic centre for Lord Justice Sir Donald Finnemore, captain of the 1st A Birmingham Company, in 1950. The are formed outside the Law Courts, Cathays Park. Tom Coakley and Dai Plank were in charge of the squad.

Newspaper boys gather in the Golate for a meeting. In 1889 newspaper boys formed themselves into a body of trade unionists after learning of plans that the proprietors of the *Evening Express* were going to sell the paper at a lower price than the *South Wales Echo*.

The *South Wales News* staff dance, 1928. The paper folded shortly afterwards in that year.

South Wales Echo v. Bristol Evening Post, 1933. This is believed to be the first football team to travel to a match by air transport. The *Echo* won the match. Left to right, back row: Patsy O' Connel, Bert Ovens, Fred Dark, Billy MacKelvie, Gus Perriam, -?-,Chris Godwin, Dennis Donovan, Sammy Ovens. Front row: Frank Gwyn, Norman Hall, Jerry Parle, Charlie Harry, Ray Pointer, Ginger Murray.

Western Mail rugby team annual dinner at the Globe Hotel, *c.* 1952. John Billot, who later became the paper's sports editor, is pictured fourth from the right on the back row.

The last Cardiff tram, 1950. The banner reads, 'Goodbye my friends this is the end I've travelled miles and miles and watched your faces through the years show anger, tears & smiles. Although you've criticised my looks & said I was too slow. I got you there and brought you back through rain, sleet & snow.' The tram service had run since 1902, totalling forty-eight years service.

Former patients and nurses from Sully Hospital met in the Castle Arcade in 1964 to record a song to be played on the hospital's radio programme. The song was called *Hello Sully* and it was sung to the tune of *Hello Dolly*. Among the patients are Jacqueline Lee, Betty Williams and Doreen Lippert.

Six
Civic Functions

A Royal Salute for the Queen's birthday outside the elegant City Hall, *c.* 1985.

Bill Surringer, the First Macebearer, *c.* 1985. He met many famous people in his role as First Macebearer, including Princess Diana, but he is seen here meeting Wales's own Tom Jones.

Bill Surringer at his desk in the City Hall, *c.* 1990. His autograph book is full of the names of famous people, from Tom Jones (above) to John Conteh (see p. 127).

Dignitaries in the City Hall in 1993. They are, left to right: Colonel Sam Smith, Lady Mayoress Mrs Riley, Lord Mayor and Councillor Riley, Chief Executive Roger Payne, Bill Surringer the Lord Mayor City Officer and First Macebearer.

The Prince of Wales signing the VIP visitors' book at Cardiff Castle in 1994. Included are: Lloyd Edwards, Harry Poloway (toast master), the Lady Mayoress, Recorder Judge Gibbon, Lord Mayor Ricky Ormonde, Bill Surringer.

The Prince of Wales (third left, talking to the Lord Mayor Ricky Ormonde and Lady Mayoress) leaving Cardiff Castle after signing the VIP visitors' book in 1994.

The Prince of Wales with the Lord Mayor, Tim Davies, on a visit to Cardiff in 1995.

The freedom of the city was presented to the South Wales Area of the National Union of Mineworkers on 1 April 1995. The mineworkers were granted a resolution which, on the motion of Cllr W.P. Herbert and seconded by Cllr P.W. Morris, was passed by the council at a special meeting held on 27 July 1994. It gave them 'the privilege, honour and distinction of marching through the streets of Cardiff, the Capital of Wales, on ceremonial occasions with banners flying and bands playing'.

A Cardiff Castle function, *c.* 1995. Left to right: Bill Surringer, Harry Poloway, Brian Rix, Bob Morgan.

Lord Mayor Max Phillips leaving Cardiff Castle led by macebearers Bill Surringer and Bob Morgan in 1997.

The St Johns Ambulance annual assembly walk from the City Hall to Cardiff Castle in 1997. Macebearers Bill Surringer and Bob Morgan lead the way for Lord Mayor Max Phillips.

Macebearers Bill Surringer and Bob Morgan head a parade of city dignitaries.

Champion boxer John Conteh
shaking hands with Bill Surringer
in July 1995.

Brian Lee.

Acknowledgements

I am greatly indebted to the editors of *The Western Mail*, *South Wales Echo* and *Cardiff Post* for their help once again. They not only published my requests to their readers for photographs, but were kind enough to give me permission to use some of their own. As a young lad, I once sold the *Echo* and little did I think then that one day I would be writing, at one time or another, a column for all three publications.

For the loan of photographs I must thank: Idris John, Jim Davies, Mrs Cleary, Norman Hopkins, Phil Street, Peter Narusberg, George Frantzeskou of Cardiff County Council's Leisure and Sports Department, John Sweeney, Allen Hambly, Tracy Wiltshire of Cardiff and County Council's Planning Department, John Billot former sports editor of *The Western Mail*, Malcolm Collins, Peter Person, Valerie and Malcolm Beames, Sally Uphill of the Commercial Photography department, Western Mail & Echo Ltd, Lennie and Meg Johnson, Neil Jones who took the Civic Functions pictures, David Davies, FRICS of Stephenson & Alexander, High Street, Cardiff .

For their continuing support I would like to thank Bill Barrett, who writes the widely read 'My Cardiff' column in the *Cardiff Post*, and Gina Groom of Wales in Action. I would also like to thank my son-in-law Russell Harvey and grandson James Lee Harvey for setting up and installing the computer on which the text for this book has been processed . For writing the foreword my special thanks go to John Billot one of the nicest people it has been my pleasure to meet. Special thanks to my editor, Jane Friel, for her helpful suggestions concerning the layout and advice on some of the text. Thanks also to the staff of the Local Studies department of the Central Library for their help.

Finally, my sincere thanks to all those people who offered photographs which, for one reason or another were not used, and ask forgiveness of anyone I may have inadvertently omitted from these acknowledgements.